Australian Cattle Dogs

Paige V. Polinsky

Checkerboard
Library

An Imprint of Abdo Publishing
abdopublishing.com

abdopublishing.com

Published by Abdo Publishing, a division of ABDO, PO Box 398166, Minneapolis, MN 55439.
Copyright © 2017 by Abdo Consulting Group, Inc. International copyrights reserved in all
countries. No part of this book may be reproduced in any form without written permission from
the publisher. Checkerboard Library™ is a trademark and logo of Abdo Publishing.

Printed in the United States of America, North Mankato, Minnesota.
062016
092016

**THIS BOOK CONTAINS
RECYCLED MATERIALS**

Cover Photo: Shutterstock
Interior Photos: Animal Photography/Sally Anne Thompson, p. 7; Shutterstock, pp. 1, 5, 9, 10, 11,
    13, 15, 16–17, 19, 21

Series Coordinator: Tamara L. Britton
Editor: Liz Salzmann
Production: Mighty Media, Inc.

Library of Congress Cataloging-in-Publication Data

Names: Polinsky, Paige V., author.
Title: Australian cattle dogs / Paige V. Polinsky.
Description: Minneapolis, MN : Abdo Publishing, [2017] | Series: Dogs ; set
    13 | Includes index.
Identifiers: LCCN 2016007740 (print) | LCCN 2016017137 (ebook) | ISBN
    9781680781748 (print) | ISBN 9781680775594 (ebook)
Subjects: LCSH: Australian cattle dog--Juvenile literature. | Herding
    dogs--Juvenile literature. | Dog breeds--Juvenile literature.
Classification: LCC SF429.A77 P65 2016 (print) | LCC SF429.A77 (ebook) | DDC
    636.737--dc23
LC record available at https://lccn.loc.gov/2016007740

Contents

The Dog Family

You have probably heard the phrase "man's best friend." But did you know that this friendship is thousands of years old? The first **domesticated** dogs protected humans and helped them hunt. In return, the dogs received food and shelter.

Scientists believe these dogs descended from the gray wolf. But dogs have come a long way since then. There are now more than 400 dog **breeds** worldwide! They are all members of the family **Canidae**. Coyotes, wolves, and dingoes belong to this family too.

Today's dogs come in many different shapes, colors, and sizes. Many are solely companions, but some have special jobs. The Australian cattle dog (ACD) is a fun, lively companion. But this hardworking breed is also great at herding livestock.

The Australian cattle dog resembles its ancestor, the dingo.

Australian Cattle Dogs

In the 1800s, Australian settlers needed a strong herding dog. The dog had to be able to drive cattle long distances. A man named George Elliott began **breeding** Scotch collies with dingoes. The resulting dogs were very hardworking and popular.

Two decades later, brothers Jack and Harry Bagust wanted to improve Elliott's breed. They bred Elliott's dogs with Dalmatians and Australian kelpies. The new breed was the Australian cattle dog.

ACDs were excellent herders. They were tough and determined and worked well with cattle. ACDs helped cattle ranchers manage much larger herds. The **American Kennel Club (AKC)** recognized the ACD as an official breed in 1980.

Farmers around the world use Australian cattle dogs to watch over their cattle.

What They're Like

If you're a high-energy adventure seeker, then the ACD is for you! This rough-and-tumble working dog hates to sit still. The ACD was **bred** for long hours of hard labor. This makes it perfect for farmers, athletes, and outdoor enthusiasts. Without a challenging job, it can become bored and destructive.

But the ACD is more than just active. It is highly intelligent and eager to learn. As a natural watchdog, it is wary of strangers. But it is loyal, loving, and faithful to its family. Once you earn its trust, you have a friend for life.

In order to control large herds, the ACD must be stubborn and forceful. It has even been known to nip at people's heels! These dogs can be especially

Brave ACDs love to explore the great outdoors.

bossy toward children. Firm, positive training can help prevent this. The **breed** behaves best with children with whom it was raised.

Coat and Color

ACD fur is beautiful, low maintenance, and even weatherproof! This **breed** has a short, smooth double coat. The straight top layer lies flat against the body. It is resistant to rain and dirt. The bottom layer is the undercoat. It is short and **dense**.

Every ACD **sheds** its undercoat once or twice a year. Year-round, it sheds a moderate amount. Weekly brushing can help keep this under control.

This breed's hardy fur can be blue or red. The blue ACD has a solid or speckled blue coat. Its legs, chest, throat, and jaw

are partly tan. It has blue, black, or tan markings on its head. Some have a black "single mask" over one eye, resembling a pirate's eye patch!

The red ACD looks more similar to its dingo ancestors. Its red fur is evenly speckled. Some have darker red markings on their heads.

ACDs are also called red heelers (*left*) or blue heelers.

Size

The ACD is muscular and medium in size. Females stand 17 to 19 inches (43 to 48 cm) tall. Males generally measure 18 to 20 inches (46 to 51 cm) in height. Both males and females weigh 35 to 45 pounds (16 to 20 kg).

This **breed** is built for speed, strength, and **endurance**. It has a compact, rectangular body with powerful shoulders and a deep chest. Its long, thick tail is slightly curved. When running, the ACD uses its tail as a **rudder** for quick direction changes!

The ACD has a broad head and medium-length **muzzle**. Its ears are pointed and stand up. It has a strong jaw for nipping cattle. Its alert, dark-brown eyes are known to look suspiciously at strangers. But ACDs are better recognized for their wide, friendly smiles!

The ACD's physical abilities serve it well for herding work.

Care

The ACD is generally quite robust. But they do have a history of deafness and blindness. Take your ACD to a veterinarian for regular checkups. The vet will check your dog's eyes and ears. The vet can also give **vaccines** and **spay** or **neuter** your dog.

Minimal grooming will keep your ACD looking and feeling great! Because of its dirt-resistant coat, it won't need baths often. But you should brush its fur weekly and trim its nails each month.

Did you know that there is special toothpaste for dogs? Brush your ACD's teeth regularly to prevent tooth decay. You should also check its ears for infection. Begin these **routines** when your dog is still a puppy to help it adjust.

Make sure your dog gets a lot of activity. An ACD needs at least two to three hours of exercise each day!

The ACD's active lifestyle can be muddy! But its coat is easy to care for.

Feeding

A healthy diet is very important for keeping your ACD energized! And there are many quality dry, semi-moist, and wet foods. The amount of food your dog needs can vary. Your vet can give you instructions based on your dog's age, size, and lifestyle.

Your ACD puppy will need a lot of food to grow. It should eat about three meals each day. Feed your dog the same food as its **breeder** did to avoid an upset tummy.

Your adult ACD should generally eat one to two meals per day. Avoid making sudden changes to your dog's food. And make sure it always has fresh water to drink. Your dog will be extra thirsty from all of its exercise!

A glossy coat is just one benefit of a balanced diet.

Treats are useful for training, but give them in moderation. Most importantly, do not overfeed your ACD. **Obesity** can cause **kidney** disease, breathing problems, and a shorter life span. It will prevent your ACD from doing the activities it loves. A healthy diet will keep your dog fit and active.

Things They Need

The ACD was born to boss cattle around. Without a firm leader, it might try to boss you too! But with patience and steady training, its **obedience** is legendary.

Your pup will also need lots of love and attention. It will want to be with you wherever you go. That is why many people call the ACD a "**Velcro** dog"!

No ACD wants to sit inside all day. And you don't need cattle to exercise your dog! The ACD is excellent at dog sports, such as **agility** and flying disc competitions. It is also a great running, biking, and hiking companion.

You will need some basic supplies to care for your ACD. You will need to buy a leash and collar.

Identification tags are especially important in case your ACD gets lost. And a comfortable crate is a nice place for it to rest. It will also appreciate a fun selection of chew toys!

Australian cattle dogs shine in agility competitions, such as the bar jump!

Puppies

Like most dogs, a mother ACD is **pregnant** for about 63 days. She has a **litter** of five to seven puppies. ACD puppies are born white, blind, and deaf. Their eyes and ears begin working after two weeks. As they get older, their fur color changes.

At eight weeks old, the puppies can leave their mother. But take your time choosing your ACD puppy! Contact a **reputable** shelter or **breeder**. Ask about the health of the dog's parents. Then get to know your puppy before you bring it home.

You should start training your ACD as soon as possible. **Socialize** it with other animals, people, and children. Teach it not to nip. Give your puppy lots of love, patience, and guidance. And prepare to enjoy 12 to 16 years of ACD adventure!

Puppy kindergarten classes are a great way to train young ACDs.

Glossary

agility - a sport in which a handler leads a dog through an obstacle course during a timed race.

American Kennel Club (AKC) - an organization that studies and promotes interest in purebred dogs.

breed - a group of animals sharing the same ancestors and appearance. A breeder is a person who raises animals. Raising animals is often called breeding them.

Canidae (KAN-uh-dee) - the scientific Latin name for the dog family. Members of this family are called canids. They include wolves, jackals, foxes, coyotes, and domestic dogs.

dense - thick or compact.

domesticated - adapted to life with humans.

endurance - the ability to sustain a long, stressful effort or activity.

kidney - one of a pair of organs that help the body get rid of waste products.

litter - all of the puppies born at one time to a mother dog.

muzzle - an animal's nose and jaws.

neuter (NOO-tuhr) - to remove a male animal's reproductive glands.

obedience - the quality of doing what one is told to do.

obesity - the condition of having too much body fat.

pregnant - having one or more babies growing within the body.

reputable - respected and trusted by most people.

routine - a regular order of actions or way of doing something.

rudder - a blade on the bottom of a boat near the back. When moved, it causes the boat to turn.

shed - to cast off hair, feathers, skin, or other coverings or parts by a natural process.

socialize - to adapt an animal to behaving properly around people or other animals in various settings.

spay - to remove a female animal's reproductive organs.

vaccine (vak-SEEN) - a shot given to prevent illness or disease.

Velcro - the brand name of a type of fabric that has two sides that stick together.

Websites

To learn more about Dogs, visit **booklinks.abdopublishing.com**. These links are routinely monitored and updated to provide the most current information available.

Index